BALLOON ARCHITECTURE

D1298068

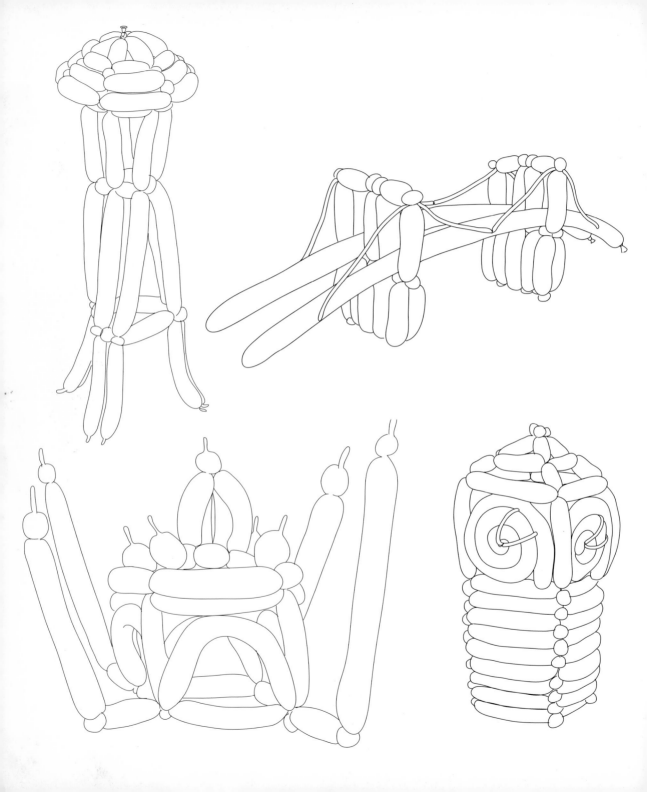

BALLOON ARCHITECTURE

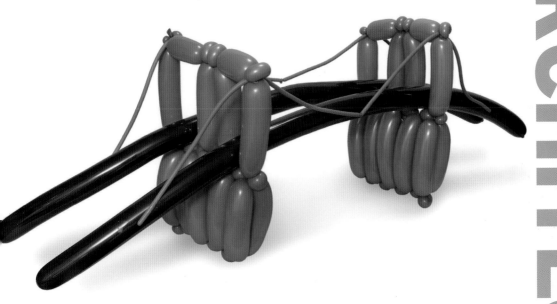

CONSTRUCT THE WORLD'S
10 COOLEST BUILDINGS

Larry Moss

METRO BOOKS
NEW YORK

This 2007 edition published by Metro Books,
by arrangement with Ivy Press.

Metro Books
122 Fifth Avenue
New York, NY 10011

ISBN-13: 978-0-7607-9285-8
ISBN-10: 0-7607-9285-2

Library of Congress Cataloging-in-Publication data available

Printed and bound in China

10 9 8 7 6 5 4 3   -

This book was conceived, designed, and produced
by iBall, an imprint of Ivy Press
The Old Candlemakers, West Street,
Lewes, East Sussex BN7 2NZ, U.K.

Creative Director Peter Bridgewater
Publisher Jason Hook
Editorial Director Caroline Earle
Art Director Sarah Howerd
Senior Project Editor Mary Todd
Designer Clare Barber
Photography Pat St. Clair
Illustrations Ivan Hissey

CONTENTS

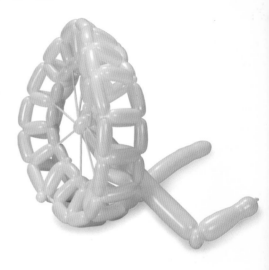

INTRODUCTION

The materials we use for building evolve as technology advances. Some materials are stronger, more energy efficient, or easier to use. Others offer no benefits to the builder whatsoever. They have less energy efficiency, won't stand up to the weather, and won't even last for more than a few days without exceptional treatment. That's where balloon art (I like to call it "airigami") comes in. The frailness of balloons and their temporary nature are part of what makes them so much fun to use.

In this book, things are made easy because other designers have already done the hard part and provided something to copy. By selecting some of the world's most famous buildings, we only have to create things that hint at the original to stir up a feeling of recognition. With enough time and materials, we could reproduce even the tiniest of details in the most elaborate buildings. However, the goal of this book is not to build full-scale replicas, indistinguishable from the originals. It is to abstract the buildings you are familiar with so that you can finish each structure in a short time.

Great effort went into ensuring that all the structures in this book can be built with only a handful of balloons. However, once you understand the basics, you can take things to extremes. Experiment with colors, add more detail to the landmarks shown here or go even further and build a full-size house that people can walk into. I've constructed fairy-tale buildings like castles, the houses of the three little pigs, playground equipment, and other fun structures that are large enough for kids of all ages to explore inside and out.

My own pet project is even larger. Using only balloons (tens of thousands of them), I led a crew of 300 volunteers in building a ten-room, family-friendly haunted house in Rochester, NY, called Balloon Manor. By the time this book is published, the Manor will have reappeared, this time using almost 100,000 balloons.

Build, explore, and enjoy balloons as a medium for artistic expression. There are examples all around you that you can copy or even improve on with a little bit of imagination!

ABOUT BALLOONS

Balloons come in every imaginable shape and size. These days, a variety of materials are used to make balloons, including latex rubber, plastic, foil, and paper. Any balloon can be used as part of some elaborate creation. This book focuses on latex rubber balloons only, in a few sizes.

BEE BODY (321)

TWISTY BALLOON (260)

SPAGHETTI BALLOON (160)

BALLOON TYPES

The balloons used most often for twisted creations are the long, skinny variety, often called "twisty balloons." Most of the buildings in this book use twisty balloons that are approximately 2 inches (5 cm) in diameter by 60 inches (1.5 m) when fully inflated. This type of balloon is often called a 260 and is frequently referred to by older instructional books as a "pencil balloon."

Some of the sculptures here were designed using an even narrower balloon of about 1 inch (2.5 cm) by 60 inches (1.5 m), or a 160. These are sometimes referred to as "spaghetti balloons."

BEE BODY BALLOONS

The last balloon type used in this book—the 321—has a more unique shape. It's about 3 inches (7.5 cm) in diameter, can easily be inflated to about 9 inches (23 cm), and has a differently colored point at the end that is not intended to be inflated. Balloon artists have named this balloon a "bee body" since it's a natural shape to represent a bee with a stinger on the end. While its insect appearance isn't of importance in this book, its shape does make it useful for creating the spires on some buildings, such as the Taj Mahal.

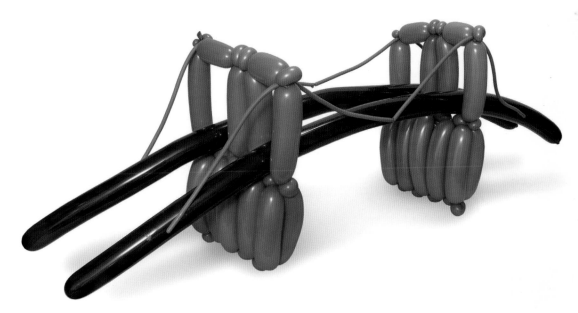

WORKING WITH BALLOONS

Many other balloon types and sizes exist along the continuum, from spaghetti balloons to the round or spherical party balloons we see all the time. Some balloons form recognizable figures as soon as they are inflated. All latex rubber balloons, no matter what their shape when they come out of the bag, can be twisted, bent, squeezed, and otherwise abused by the artist. The balloons used to make the sculptures in this book were chosen for a variety of reasons. Usually it was to make a given sculpture easier for someone tackling it for the first time. Feel free to experiment with whatever balloon sizes you have available. Sometimes "bubble sizes" will need to be adjusted to suit different sizes of balloon. Usually when fatter balloons are used, fewer twists can be placed in them, resulting in the need for more balloons in a sculpture. By experimenting a little, you'll quickly learn the characteristics of the different types of balloon.

INFLATING THE BALLOONS

Inflating the balloons is probably the hardest part of creating balloon art. Most balloon artists, whether hobbyists or pros, attempt mouth inflation. Feel free to try it, but don't waste too much time on it. That's what pumps are for!

PUMPS

Just about any kind of air pump can be used. The only requirement is that there is a nozzle on the pump that the neck of the balloon will fit over. There are pumps made specifically for balloons. These tend to be somewhat easier to work with, but some ball pumps and bicycle tire pumps can be used quite successfully.

GENERAL TIPS FOR INFLATING BALLOONS

• Always leave space at the end of the balloon with no air in it. As shapes are made, air will be pushed into the empty area.

• For certain twists it may be helpful to let a bit of air out of the balloon before you tie the knot. This is known as "burping" the balloon. This will soften the balloon, make it easier to work with, and reduce the risk of popping. Letting too much air out of the balloon will make it difficult for the sculpture to hold its shape.

• When using a pump, you may find that the balloon feels very stiff when it is inflated. After you let a little air out, squeeze the balloon lightly along its entire length to soften it.

• If you release all of the air from a balloon and then reinflate it, it will be fatter than before, so reusing balloons is generally not a good idea.

• If you want a longer balloon than you have, it is possible to gently stretch an inflated balloon.

POPPING

Balloons do not pop very often if you're careful, but they will pop. It's best to get used to it rather than worrying about it. You should keep balloons away from sensitive areas like your eyes, but generally a balloon popping doesn't hurt you—it just makes a loud, unexpected noise. As you become proficient at sculpting, fewer will burst. Using fresher and better quality balloons will help to an extent, but nothing helps more than practice.

REPAIRS

Repairing sculptures with popped sections can be easy if you've lost a single accessible bubble, or more time-consuming than starting over if the lost section was critical to structural integrity. In a larger sculpture, a popped bubble generally isn't noticeable and can be ignored. If a bubble pops after a sculpture is completed, assess the situation to determine whether it is worth the risk of attempting a repair. If you do attempt a repair, be very careful that, by touching the popped area, you aren't setting off a chain reaction and releasing air from other connected sections. When a balloon pops while you're in the process of making a sculpture, tying in a new balloon is usually a simple task. To do this, follow the three steps below:

1 Hold the popped section in one hand so the balloon doesn't inflate while you ready another balloon to tie in.

2 Tie the nozzle end of the new balloon to the broken piece of balloon.

3 Once attached, the nozzle and knot are hidden by the twist.

TYING THE BALLOONS

There are no special knots required to keep the air in a balloon. A basic overhand knot works fine. Many methods of tying even the simplest of knots exist. If you find you have difficulty, the following is a simple approach.

1 Hold the nozzle of the balloon between thumb and forefinger.

2 Stretch and wrap the nozzle of the balloon around your forefinger and middle finger. Keeping space between the two fingers as you do this will make the next step easier.

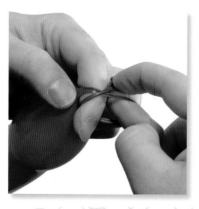

3 Complete the overhand knot by inserting the nozzle through the opening between your fingers.

4 Pull the nozzle through as you slip the balloon carefully off your fingers.

5 Pull securely, but don't tug on the knot, as pulling too tightly will only tear the balloon.

LENGTHENING THE NOZZLE

If you find the nozzle of the balloon isn't long enough for you to wrap around a couple of fingers, you can release air from the end of the balloon. To do this:

1 Form a small bubble in the balloon by putting a twist in it.

2 Release air from the bubble while pinching the balloon at the twist.

BASIC TWISTS

You may already have tried to twist a balloon and found that your twists just won't stay. It's the pressure and friction between bubbles that forces them to hold their shape. One bubble alone will untwist, returning the balloon to its pre-twisted state. Only a few basic twists are needed for all the sculptures presented here.

FOLD TWIST

1 Fold an inflated balloon anywhere.

2 Pinch the doubled section of the balloon.

3 Hold the two free ends of the balloon while twisting the folded section several times.

4 Release the balloon and see how the folded sections hold together securely.

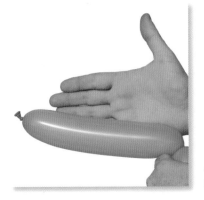

A hand's-length bubble.

BUBBLE SIZES

Bubble sizes throughout this book are given as imprecise terms, such as "long" and "short." Where more precision is needed, you'll see bubble sizes indicated by measurements against parts of the body like hands and fingers. This vagueness is not intended to create mystery or frustration for the balloon artist.

Greater frustration would be encountered by newcomers to the art if attempts were made to give precise measurements. You could sit with a ruler and follow instructions exactly and still find that your creations differed from the ones in the photos. Everyone handles balloons differently, applying pressure with slight variation. As a result, measurements will never be exactly the same when a sculpture is made by different people. Work with the balloons and get used to using your fingers to measure. Your fingers are already touching the balloons anyway. It's far easier to use them than to pick up an extra measuring device.

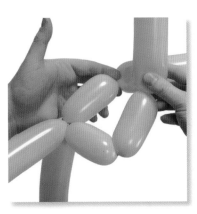

Hand's-width bubbles.

PINCH AND LOCK TWIST

1 Pinch the balloon between your thumb and forefinger.

2 Twist the bubble around several times.

3 Use two fingers to hold the first twist you've made. Now pinch and twist the balloon again, forming a second bubble.

4 Make sure the second, and all subsequent bubbles, are twisted in the same direction and the same number of times. This ensures that, as long as you hold the first and last bubbles in a sequence, none of the bubbles will untwist.

5 Continue to hold the first twist between your fingers while you reach further down the balloon and form another bubble.

6 Make sure to hold the first and last twists in a sequence. By doing this, the whole chain of bubbles will hold.

7 Fold the balloon so the last two bubbles you made are sitting alongside each other.

9 The pinch and lock twist is now complete.

8 With the ends of the bubbles lined up, twist and lock those bubbles together.

PINCH TWIST

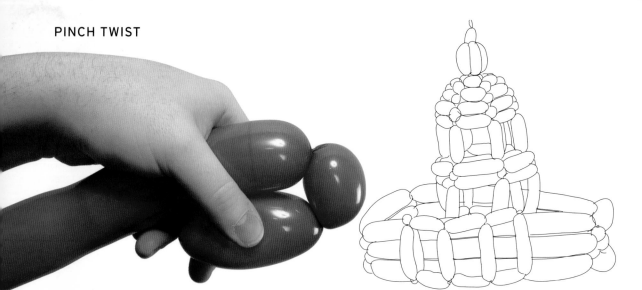

1 Make two small bubbles and fold the balloon so that the first bubble sits alongside the remaining length of balloon.

TIP

You may find that your hand tires from twisting so many bubbles in a complex sculpture. It is a good idea to switch the hand that does the twisting from time to time, but make sure your twists continue to go in the same direction.

2 Pull the center of the middle bubble outward.

3 Twist the center so the two ends of the bubble can meet and lock together.

TULIP TWIST

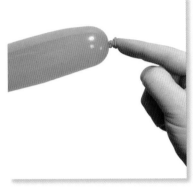

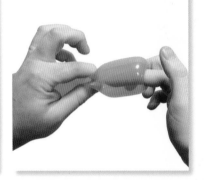

1 Place the index finger of one hand on the knot of the balloon.

2 Push the knot inside the balloon until it covers about two-thirds of your finger.

3 Grab the knot through the balloon with your other hand.

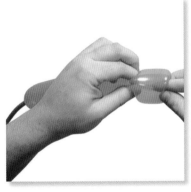

5 Keep holding the knot while you twist the bubble.

4 While holding the knot, work your index finger slowly out of the balloon.

THE PROJECTS

Twisting balloons is like drawing and painting. You don't start out creating the *Mona Lisa*. You work up to it, learning from each creation as you go. The models in this book have been carefully chosen and arranged so you progress gradually to more complex structures. Each model has something new to offer. Try to work through all of them, paying attention to the techniques, rather than simply the "recipes." This way you'll find that the models get easier to build as you progress.

EIFFEL TOWER

Once called an "eyesore" by many people, the Eiffel Tower has become a symbol of Paris. The simple design makes it easy to create with basic modeling balloons. The tower has changed color 17 times since it was built, from red-brown through yellow-ocher, to chestnut brown, bronze and finally brownish-gray.

YOU WILL NEED

12 BLUE 260s

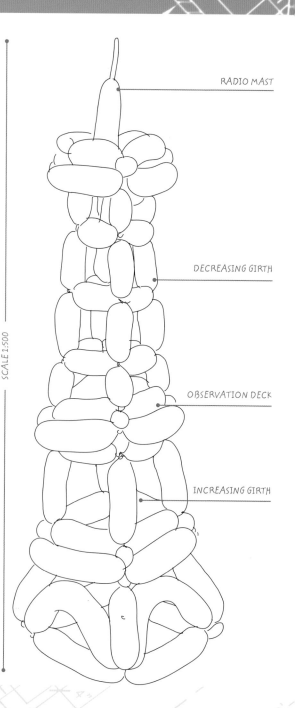

RADIO MAST

DECREASING GIRTH

SCALE 1:500

OBSERVATION DECK

INCREASING GIRTH

2 Attach the second balloon to the first by making a small bubble in the second balloon. Then join it with the twist in the first balloon.

1 Start by inflating four blue 260s, leaving only a short, uninflated nipple in each. Make the first bubble slightly longer than your hand.

3 Repeat Step 2 with the next two balloons.

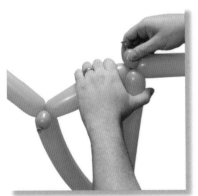

4 Join the fourth balloon to the first, forming a complete base for the tower.

5 Make a bubble long enough to form an arch from one corner of the base to another, using one of the free lengths of balloon.

6 Follow Step 5 again with the other balloons.

7 Make two bubbles in each corner balloon. Connect them to the balloon in the next corner.

8 Notice how Bubble 1 and Bubble 3 on opposite sides of the arch are joined by Bubble 2.

9 Continue all the way around, so there's a frame for each arch. You can also see this as creating a square smaller than the initial base we constructed in Step 4.

10 Cut off and tie the tail ends of the balloons.

11 Push the arches into the frames created.

12 This is the finished result. With practice, you'll be able to make all bubbles the right sizes so that the pressure between them will hold everything in place. If you have any trouble, a dab of rubber cement may be used.

13 Attach a balloon where you cut off the unusable ends of the initial balloons.

14 Then repeat the process with three more balloons, attaching one to each corner.

TIP

Make sure that you "burp" your balloon so that the air remains a flexible friend, not an explosive device. Ensure that nobody who might be offended by burping noises is present when you perform this maneuver!

15 Building the rest of the tower is almost identical to everything done so far. Form the first observation deck by making a small bubble in each corner balloon and then one longer bubble that will be joined to the balloon in the next corner.

17 Follow the same approach to make another layer of the observation deck. This time, we'll return to smaller bubbles matching the size of those at the tops of the arches.

16 This is the result. Notice that the longer bubbles are lengthier than those sitting on the top of the arches.

18 This is the finished result of the first observation deck.

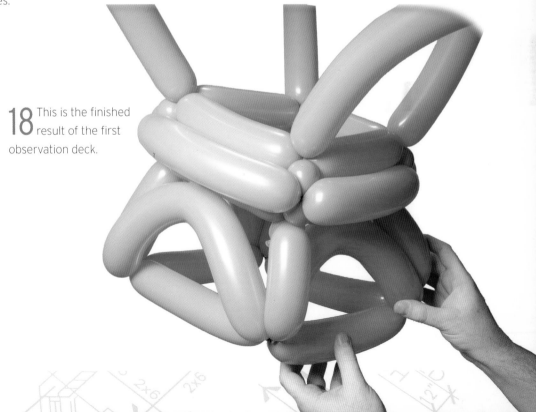

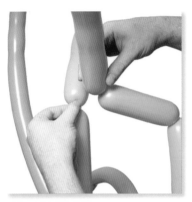

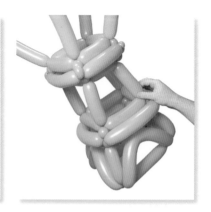

19 The pattern is repeated, with longer bubbles that separate the layers in each of the observation decks.

20 This is the finished result of the lower layer of the second observation deck.

21 Complete the second observation deck as before, adding another longer layer, then a shorter layer on top.

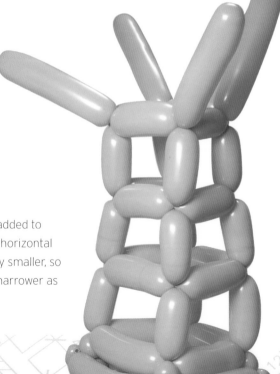

22 Continue to add more layers as before. When you reach the end of the balloons, attach four more by cutting off all the remaining unusable tails and tying in new ones.

23 As layers are added to the tower, the horizontal bubbles get gradually smaller, so the tower becomes narrower as it goes upward.

24 Add another observation deck as before.

25 Place a short piece of balloon with a long, uninflated tail into the center of the tower to create the radio mast.

FULL OF HOT AIR
In 1984, two British men parachuted off the Eiffel Tower.

BROOKLYN BRIDGE

The first steel-wire suspension bridge ever built joins Manhattan and Brooklyn. Key elements in this design are the two roadways and the arced cabling. The balloon sculpture is made in several repeatable sections.

YOU WILL NEED

14 GREEN 260s, 2 DARK BROWN 260s

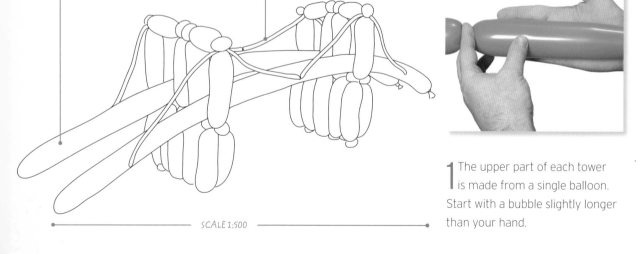

ROADWAY

ARCED CABLING

SCALE 1:500

1 The upper part of each tower is made from a single balloon. Start with a bubble slightly longer than your hand.

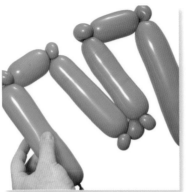

2 Make a pinch twist, followed by a bubble roughly 2 inches (5 cm) long and then another pinch twist.

3 Continue to make a series of bubbles, as shown, that will complete the upper portion of the bridge tower.

4 Use a small scrap from a popped balloon to hold together the pinch twists in the center of the tower.

5 The completed tie. Now repeat Steps 1–4 to create a second upper bridge tower.

6 Make the lower section of the tower with two balloons. Twist together a small bubble in the first balloon and a hand's-length bubble in the second.

7 Repeat Step 6 with the small bubble and the hand's-length bubbles in the opposite balloons. The overlapped bubbles are about the length of your hand.

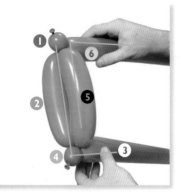

8 The bubbles in each balloon are labeled in different colors.

9 Continue to cross the balloons so they overlap each other and connect on the opposite side.

10 Do this until you have run out of balloons.

TIP

If you find it difficult to twist all the small bubbles together, use scraps of balloons wrapped around the bubbles to hold things in place.

11 Make small bubbles in the first and last bubbles of the upper tower and use these to connect to the small bubbles on the lower portion of the tower.

12 This is what the finished bridge tower looks like.

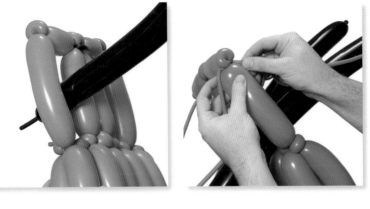

14 The cables of the bridge are formed by tying, end to end, green balloons containing just small puffs of air.

13 Insert fully inflated dark brown balloons into the gaps in the top part of the towers to form the two roadways of Brooklyn Bridge.

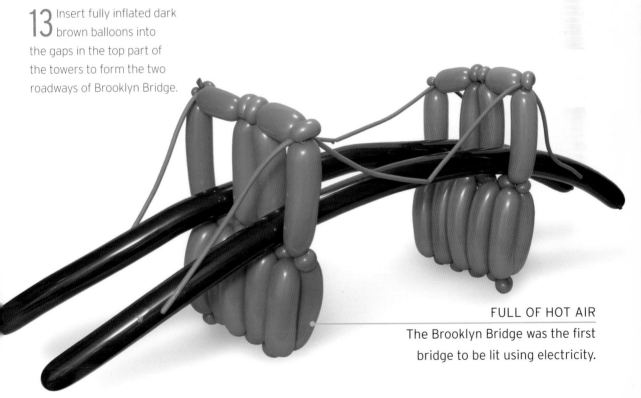

FULL OF HOT AIR
The Brooklyn Bridge was the first bridge to be lit using electricity.

GREAT PYRAMID OF GIZA

The Great Pyramid of Giza is the oldest of the Seven Wonders of the Ancient World and the only one still in existence. It is believed to have been constructed over a 20-year period concluding around 2500 BCE. The technique used here to create the regular shape of the pyramid is a very useful building block for future larger and more complex sculptures.

YOU WILL NEED

4 BLUSH OR SAND COLORED 260s

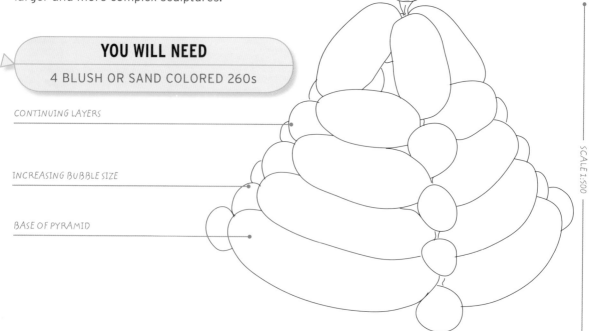

CONTINUING LAYERS

INCREASING BUBBLE SIZE

BASE OF PYRAMID

SCALE 1:500

1 Start by inflating the four balloons, leaving several inches uninflated at the end of each one. Tie the four balloons together at their nozzles.

2 In one of the balloons, make two bubbles roughly the width of your hand.

3 Make a bubble the same size in a second balloon. Then join the second twist in the first balloon with the new twist you've just made in the second balloon.

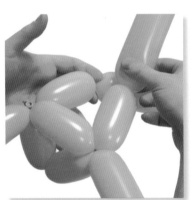

4 Repeat Steps 2 and 3 by making a bubble in the second and third balloons, also the width of your hand. The second balloon will get connected to the third.

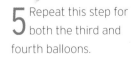

5 Repeat this step for both the third and fourth balloons.

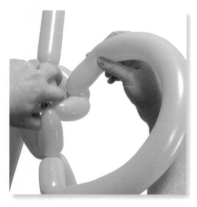

6 Eventually connect the fourth balloon back to the first.

7 This completes the top level of the pyramid.

8 Make a very small bubble in one of the balloons.

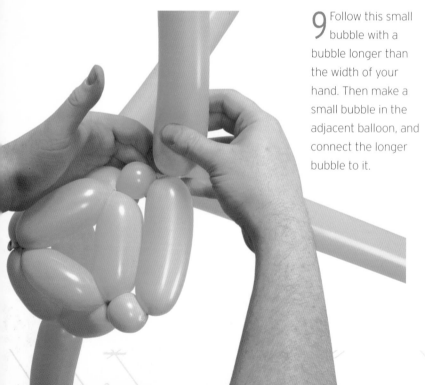

9 Follow this small bubble with a bubble longer than the width of your hand. Then make a small bubble in the adjacent balloon, and connect the longer bubble to it.

10 Continue this process and form a second layer, connecting all adjacent balloons.

TIP

If you wish to make the pyramid larger, simply tie the nozzles of four more balloons to the bottom corners of the pyramid and continue the pattern.

11 Form additional layers of the pyramid in the same way, increasing the size of the bubbles as you go.

12 Break off or deflate the tail ends of the balloons and then tie them.

FULL OF HOT AIR

The Great Pyramid of Giza was the tallest building in the world until the Eiffel Tower was built in 1889.

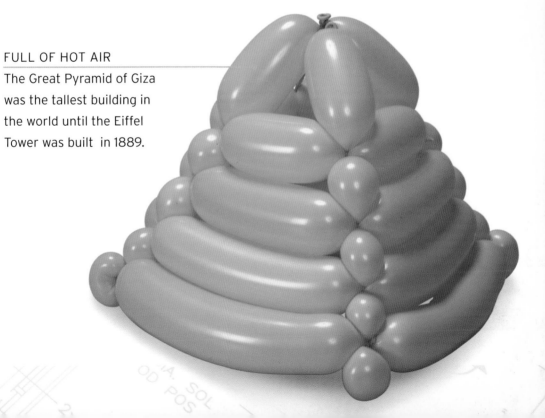

ハ. CIRADE

SPACE NEEDLE

At one time the tallest U.S. building west of the
Mississippi, Seattle's Space Needle was built for the
1962 World's Fair. Especially relevant to this book, one
of the early designs for the structure was a giant balloon
tethered to the ground.

SCALE 1:500

HEXAGON SHAPE

SUPPORTING SECTIONS

TRIPOD-STYLE BASE

YOU WILL NEED

6 GOLDENROD OR ORANGE 260s,
7 WHITE 260s

1 Inflate the six goldenrod 260s,
leaving approximately a hand's
length of uninflated tail in each
balloon. Tie the nozzles of the
six balloons together.

2 In one balloon, create two bubbles the width of your hand. In a second balloon, make a bubble the same size. Connect the first and second balloons at the last twists you formed.

3 Connect all adjacent balloons in the same manner, forming a hexagon shape.

4 Form another larger hexagon by following the same pattern. In each balloon, make a small bubble and then a larger one. The end of each larger bubble connects to the end of the smaller one in the next adjacent balloon.

6 Now create a fifth hexagon the same size as the first.

5 Make a third hexagon, larger still. Then add a fourth hexagon with smaller bubbles, the size of those in the second hexagon.

7 Deflate and tie the remaining ends of the balloons.

8 Inflate six white 260s almost fully and attach them, one at a time, to the ends of the goldenrod balloons.

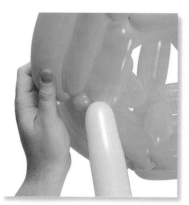

9 By twisting the nozzle of the white balloon into an existing twist or around an end bubble, the balloon will be held securely. Any remaining bubble or balloon tail can be tucked inside the saucer part of the sculpture.

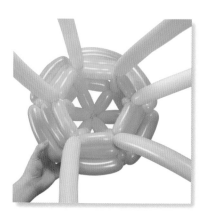

10 With the six white balloons attached, we can form the base of the building.

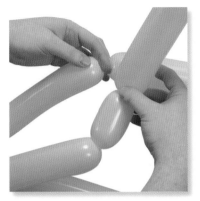

11 Use the same hexagon pattern to connect the adjacent white balloons. Make the bubbles extending away from the saucer about two hand lengths in size. Make small connecting bubbles, about the width of three fingers, between them.

12 As before, continue until all of the white balloons are joined, forming a hexagon.

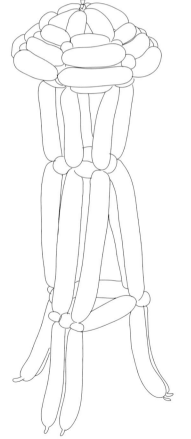

13 At this point, the lower section of the base is too flimsy to allow the sculpture to stand upright.

14 The last white balloon is needed to join the lower part of the base, turning the six legs into a kind of tripod. Tie the nozzle of the new balloon onto any of the legs.

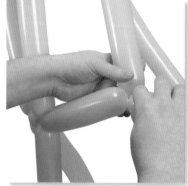

15 Make a small bubble in the new balloon and twist it onto the second leg.

16 Now use a longer bubble to connect to the third leg.

17 Alternate between long and short bubbles until you've returned to the first leg. Then break off the remaining length of balloon.

18 At this point the sculpture isn't quite stable. We can force the lowest portion of the legs to stay where we want them by forming pinch twists at the weak connection points.

19 With six pinch twists in place, one for each leg, the sculpture is far more solid.

TIP

Coins, metal washers, or other small objects can be attached to the base of these legs to weight them down and keep the sculpture from toppling.

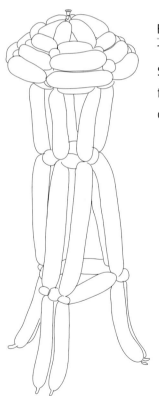

FULL OF HOT AIR

The first manager of the Space Needle suffered from acrophobia—a fear of heights!

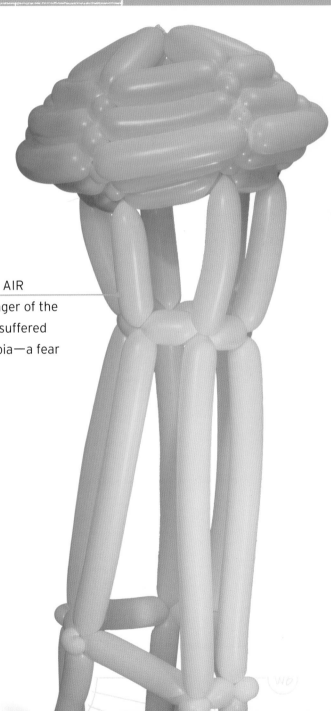

PARTHENON

The Parthenon is the most famous surviving building of ancient Greece, and dates from the 5th century BCE. Originally constructed as a temple of Athena, it was later adopted as a Christian church and an Islamic mosque.

YOU WILL NEED

8 WHITE 160s

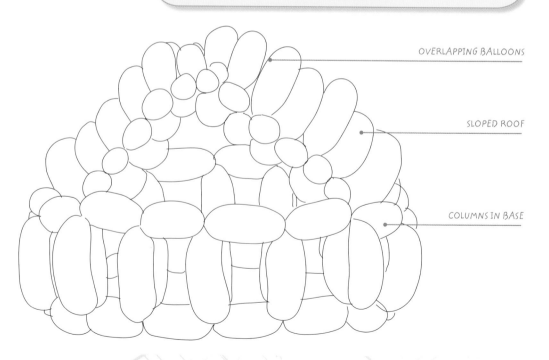

SCALE 1:500

OVERLAPPING BALLOONS

SLOPED ROOF

COLUMNS IN BASE

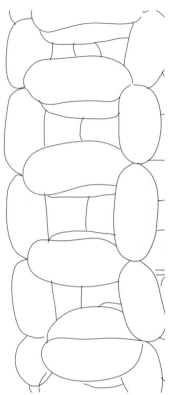

1 Inflate two 160s, leaving several inches of uninflated tail in each. Make a bubble in one of them three fingers' width in size and tie the second 160 to that bubble.

2 Make a bubble in the second balloon the same length as the bubble in the first, and tie the nozzle to the new twist you have formed. The two balloons will overlap at their ends.

3 Continue making three-finger bubble spacers and overlapping the remaining portions of the balloon until you've used up the balloons. Break off any bubbles at the end that are too short to use, and tie the ends of the balloons. The result looks like this.

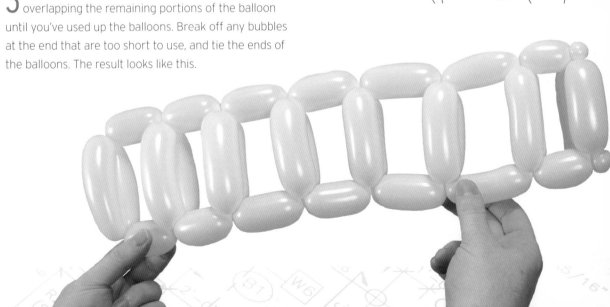

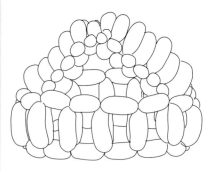

4 Tie an additional 160 to the ends of the ladder.

5 Now add one more 160 to the ladder on the other side so you can continue with the same pattern.

6 Continue the pattern until you've exhausted the length of the new balloons. Note that if you vary the lengths of the overlapping bubbles or spacer bubbles, you can change the number of columns made from two balloons.

7 Connect the end of the ladder to the starting points of the original two balloons, thus forming a large loop. This loop is the base of the Parthenon. The "rungs" of the ladder form the columns of the building.

8 The roof is made using the same pattern as the walls, but the spaces between the parallel bubbles are removed to make a solid structure. Inflate two more white 160s. Make a very small bubble in the end of one balloon and another the width of two hands in the other balloon. Twist them together.

9 Overlap the second balloon with the first. This is the same technique used to make the base of the tower in Brooklyn Bridge.

10 Continue the overlapping pattern until you've run out of balloons. This forms one side of the sloped roof.

11 With the remaining two white 160s, make a second roof section identical to the first.

12 Join the ends of the two roof sections together.

TIP

To create a larger version of this building, 260s can be used. The small 160s make it easier to get more twists out of the balloons. Try using the larger balloons to see how this changes the scale and the look of the structure.

13 Connect the ends of the roof to the top of the base.

14 Notice that only the corners of the roof are connected to the base. This forces the shape we want and the roof meets with the base.

FULL OF HOT AIR

The gigantic statue of Athena that was originally inside the Parthenon was made out of elephant ivory and gold.

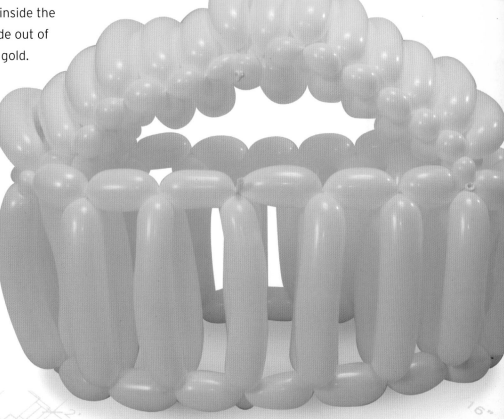

TAJ MAHAL

The Taj Mahal was built in the 17th century in Agra, India, as a mausoleum for Emperor Shah Jahan's wife. Often thought of as a single building, the Taj Mahal is actually a complex containing multiple structures.

YOU WILL NEED

5 WHITE 321s, 13 WHITE 260s

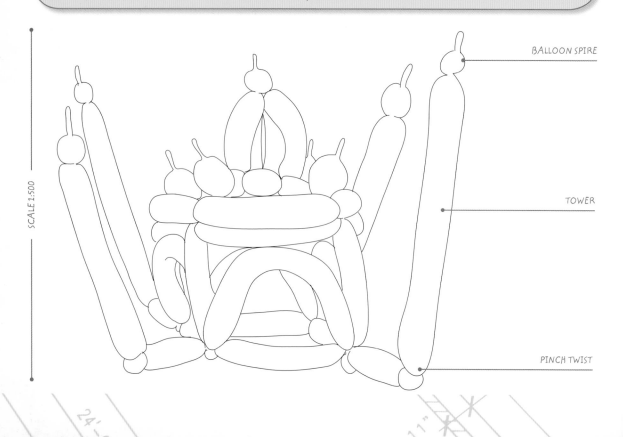

SCALE 1:500

BALLOON SPIRE

TOWER

PINCH TWIST

1 Start with four 260s, inflated and tied at their nozzles.

2 Make a bubble about two hand widths long in each of the balloons and join them together with short bubbles.

3 With all four balloons joined, we have the framework for the main dome.

4 Fill out the dome and add a spire to the top using one 321 inflated just up to the colored tip. Make a single twist an inch or so from the colored tip and insert this into the top of the dome.

5 Continue to insert the rest of the 321 into the dome with the nozzle end sticking out of the bottom.

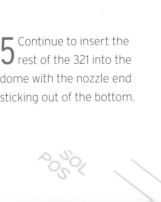

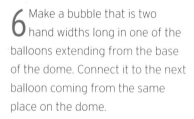
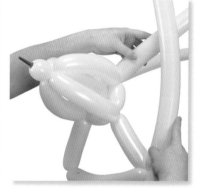

6 Make a bubble that is two hand widths long in one of the balloons extending from the base of the dome. Connect it to the next balloon coming from the same place on the dome.

7 Repeat Step 6 to create each corner of the building.

8 This forms a square around the base of the dome.

9 Make a small bubble in one of the balloons coming off the corners of the square. Tie another fully inflated 260 to that bubble.

10 Make long bubbles in the last balloon added to form another square below the first. This makes a more solid wall for the building.

11 Tie another 260 to the end of one of the corner bubbles. Then connect that new balloon to the end of the bubble at the adjacent corner.

12 Now create an arched bubble from the base of one corner to the base of the previous one. Break off any remaining lengths of balloon.

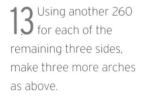

13 Using another 260 for each of the remaining three sides, make three more arches as above.

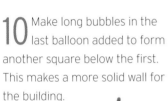

14 Partially inflate four 321s. Make a bubble near the tip of each and attach these to the four diagonal bubbles connecting the main dome to the base.

15 This is what the completed main building of the Taj Mahal complex looks like.

16 The minarets or towers are each constructed from a separate 260. Inflate the remaining four 260s, leaving a tail the width of your hand. Tie a knot at the base of the tail.

17 Push the knot into the balloon and make a tulip twist.

18 The tail of the balloon forms the spire.

19 Make a pinch twist about a hand's width from the nozzle end of the balloon.

20 The pinch twist forces the balloon into a right angle.

TIP

Pinch twists are often used to put bends into balloons and force bubbles to go in certain directions. Add pinch twists to places like the base of the arches if the bubbles don't hold quite where you want them.

21 Attach the nozzle end of the balloon to a corner of the main building. Repeat for the remaining towers.

FULL OF HOT AIR

In 1830, the Taj Mahal was scheduled to be torn down.

LONDON EYE

The London Eye, also known as the Millennium Wheel, is one of the largest observation wheels in the world. The 32 fully enclosed capsules on the wheel carry a total of 800 passengers through a 30-minute revolution. Notice how the size of the bubbles, just like structural members in a building, dictates the curve of the wheel.

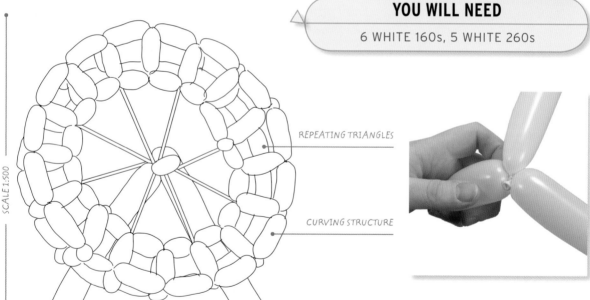

SCALE 1:500

REPEATING TRIANGLES

CURVING STRUCTURE

A-FRAME SUPPORT

YOU WILL NEED

6 WHITE 160s, 5 WHITE 260s

1 Make a bubble in a 160 equal to the width of four fingers. Tie the nozzle of a second 160 to the end of that bubble.

2 Make a four-finger bubble in the second balloon and tie a third balloon to that.

3 Make a four-finger bubble in the third balloon and tie the nozzle of the first balloon to the end of it, thus forming a triangle.

4 The triangle is the basis of the entire wheel. You'll be making many more triangles, all the same size as this one.

5 Make a three-finger bubble in the first balloon, a three-finger bubble in the second balloon, and a two-finger bubble in the third balloon as spacers for the next triangle. Then make another triangle with four-finger sides connecting the spacers.

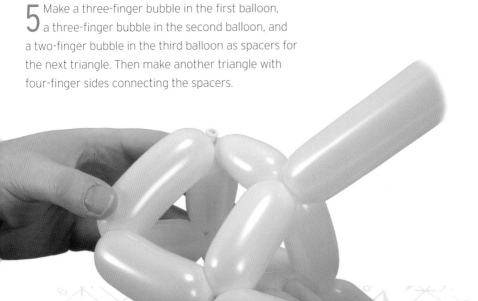

6 Continue making triangles that are all the same size with spacers as described in Step 5.

7 By continuing this pattern, with one spacer bubble always shorter than the others, you'll force your structure to curve.

8 Keep going until you reach the end of the first set of balloons. Break off any ends that are too short to use.

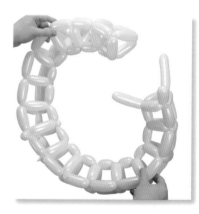

9 Attach three more 160s at the end of the semicircular frame you've made and continue the pattern further.

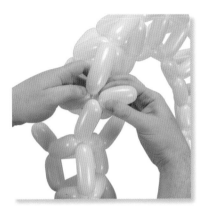

10 Now connect the ends of the 160s to the beginning of the circle.

11 Put a puff of air in a 260 and tie it. Don't inflate the balloon, just get enough air in it to make it slightly stiff.

12 Attach the end of the puffed balloon to any twisted point on the inside of the wheel.

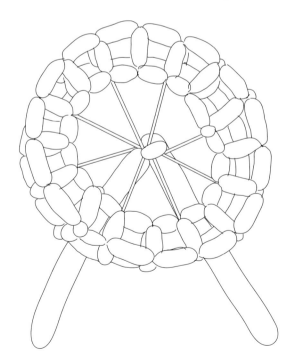

13 Stretch the puffed balloon across the wheel. Then attach it at the opposite side to form a spoke.

14 Add three more spokes, twisting them around each other in the center as you go.

15 Inflate the last 260 to use as the A-frame support for the structure. Put a pinch twist in the middle of the balloon.

16 Add a second pinch twist next to the first.

17 Slip one pinch twist from the A-frame into the center of the spokes on the wheel.

TIP

For greater detail, try creating capsules that you can attach to the outside of the wheel. Each capsule can be as simple as a small bubble made from a clear 160 balloon.

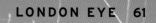

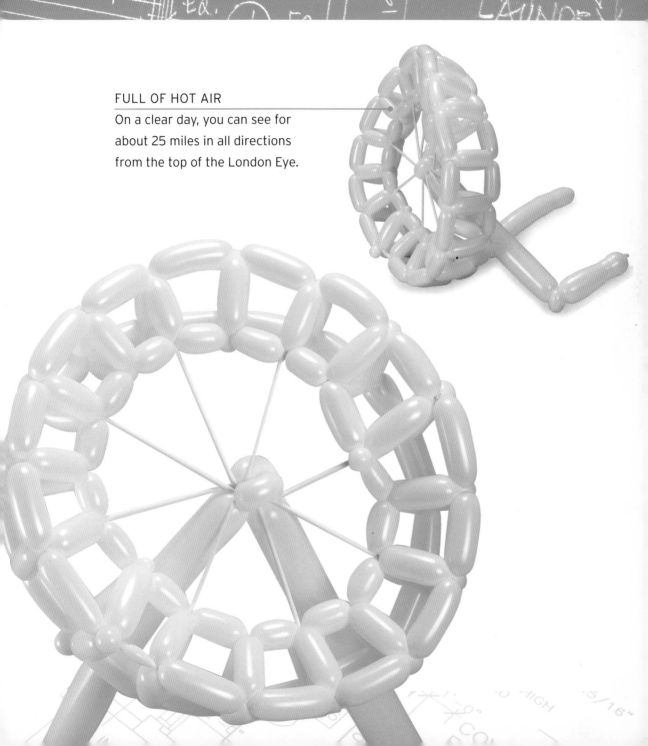

FULL OF HOT AIR

On a clear day, you can see for about 25 miles in all directions from the top of the London Eye.

TOWER BRIDGE

Tower Bridge, so named due to its proximity to the Tower of London, spans the River Thames. Its center can be opened like a drawbridge to allow river traffic to pass. The bridge opens about 100 times a year.

YOU WILL NEED

8 GREEN 260s, 2 DARK BROWN 260s, 6 LIGHT BLUE 260s, 4 GRAY 160s

SCALE 1:500

CROSSED BALLOONS

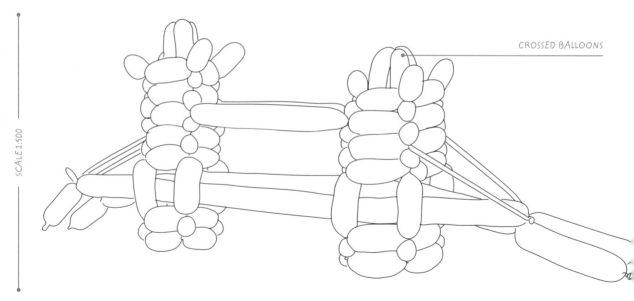

1 Inflate four green 260s and form a square with them.

2 Continue the basic pattern that you've used for other sculptures in this book to start making the first tower.

3 After the second layer, add four-finger bubble spacers before making the third layer of the tower.

4 Return to the same pattern with additional layers touching. Repeat for the second tower.

5 The completed towers have a section with a large space between layers for the road.

6 Make a cross out of two short sections of gray 160s for each of the towers.

7 Hold the crossed balloons so that the bubbles are all alongside each other. Then slide them into the top of each tower, forming a spire.

8 Fully inflate the two dark brown 260s and insert them into the base of the towers to form the roadways across the bridge.

9 Connect two sections of light blue 260s close to the tops of the towers.

10 The two blue balloons form the upper walkways.

11 Run two puffed blue 260s from the upper portion of each tower at the height of the walkways to the roadways.

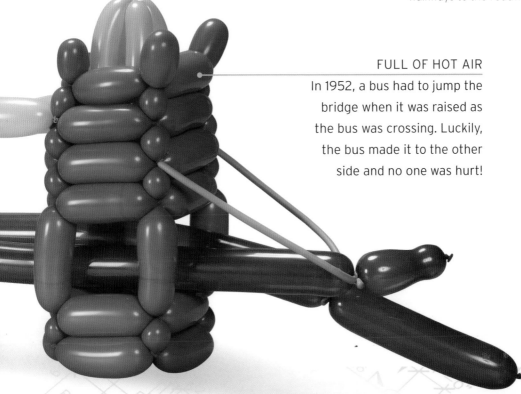

FULL OF HOT AIR

In 1952, a bus had to jump the bridge when it was raised as the bus was crossing. Luckily, the bus made it to the other side and no one was hurt!

BIG BEN

The clock tower in the Palace of Westminster, London, is the largest four-faced chiming clock in the world. The name "Big Ben" actually refers to the largest bell in the tower, although it is most often used to denote the clock and tower.

SCALE 1:500

SPIRAL CLOCK FACE

CONTINUING SQUARE PATTERN

YOU WILL NEED
4 WHITE 260s, 8 BLACK 260s, 8 BROWN 260s

1 Start with four brown 260s forming a square of about 1 foot (30.5 cm) on each side.

 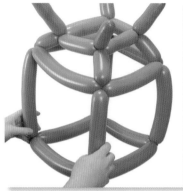 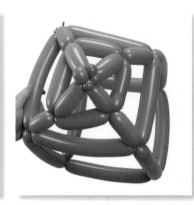

2 Make a foot-long bubble in each balloon and connect it to the adjacent balloon, forming a cube shape.

3 We want to make a point on the top of the cube. Do this by making short bubbles in each balloon and join them using smaller bubbles than those forming the sides of the cube.

4 Connect the remaining ends of the balloons, creating a peak on the tower.

5 Now a clock face needs to be added to each of the four sides of the tower.

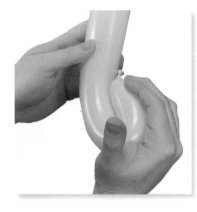

6 Fully inflate a white 260. Starting at the nozzle end, roll the balloon into a spiral.

7 Keep the spiral as tight as you can while you roll the balloon.

8 Spread your fingers around the balloon so it doesn't uncurl.

9 Position the spiraled balloon between your legs to hold it together.

10 Apply a bit of adhesive (either rubber cement, or double-sided tape) to the end of the curled balloon so that it holds its shape.

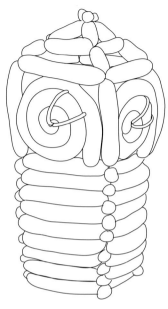

11 When the adhesive sets, the spiral will hold forming a single clock face. Repeat this three more times to create the rest of the clock faces.

12 Insert the completed spiraled balloons into the openings of the clock tower.

13 If the clock face exactly matches the size of the opening in the tower, pressure will be enough to hold it in place. A bit of adhesive will make it easier to position the clock face.

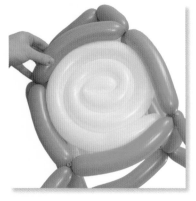

14 Attach four more brown balloons to the base of the clock tower.

15 Make a bubble the length of the clock face and attach it to a small bubble in the balloon in the adjacent corner.

16 Add layers of squares to the base of the tower with the four balloons you've attached.

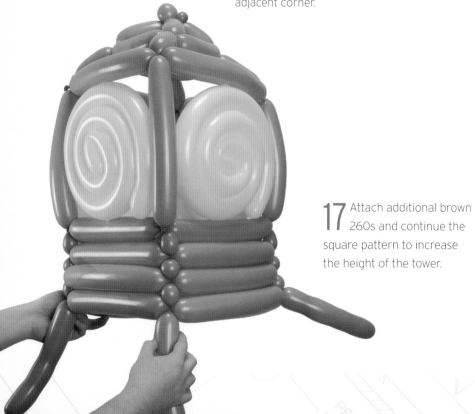

17 Attach additional brown 260s and continue the square pattern to increase the height of the tower.

TIP

Stiffer hands on the clock can be created by inserting pipe cleaners, floral wire, or popsicle sticks into balloons. These can be attached to an inexpensive clock mechanism that can be mounted on the inside of the tower, making a fully operational model of Big Ben.

18 Using puffed black 260s, add hands to the faces of the clock.

FULL OF HOT AIR

The accuracy of the clock movement in Big Ben is controlled by placing old pennies in the mechanism.

CAPITOL BUILDING

The Capitol Building is the location for the U.S. Congress in Washington, D.C. The District of Columbia is divided into quadrants, with the Capitol Building at the center of the city's grid. In this final sculpture, you'll find the box-like shape of the bridge towers, the dome-like shape of the Space Needle's saucer, and the Parthenon columns.

YOU WILL NEED

15 WHITE 160s

SCALE 1:500

CONCENTRIC CIRCLES

1 Start with six inflated 160s, tied together at the nozzles.

2 Use the circular pattern we've used before in the Space Needle's saucer to join the adjacent balloons.

3 Form three concentric circles, slowly increasing in size.

4 Make another ring the same size as the last one, but this time with longer vertical bubbles separating the new ring from the initial three.

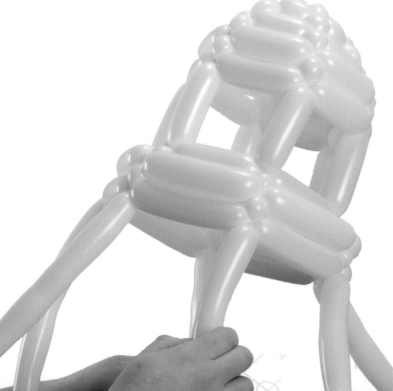

5 Make two more rings slightly larger than the last. This completes the rotunda. Place this to one side.

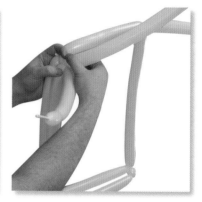

6 The rectangular portion of the building again uses the same pattern. This time, we'll start with only four 160s, almost fully inflated. Only a few twists will be made in these balloons, so don't leave too large a tail. Now join them to form a rectangle.

7 As in other sculptures with a square or rectangular base, make a small bubble in one balloon, followed by a long bubble to match the size of the bubble in the previous layer. Then join that with the next balloon.

8 Continue to make long bubbles to add another layer to the base rectangle.

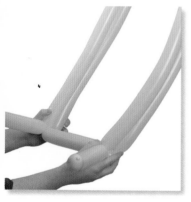

10 We want to add another layer or two to the walls, but the balloons probably aren't long enough. Instead, we'll use the remaining bubbles to add stability and provide a way to connect the rotunda. Therefore, connect the four loose ends in the center.

9 Once again, connect adjacent balloons, forming a second layer to the building.

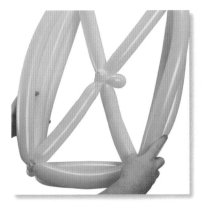

11 Attach more balloons at the four corners and add at least one more layer to the walls. Now put this section aside.

12 To put columns on the front of the building, we'll use the ladder technique we learned while making the roof of the Parthenon. Two 160s are joined together by overlapping the ends.

13 Continue in this way, overlapping the balloons, leaving space between each set of overlapped columns.

14 Once four columns are completed, break and tie off the tails of the balloons.

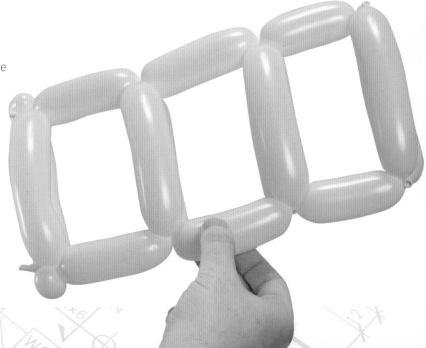

15 The columns will be placed in front of the building and affixed with a small piece of adhesive.

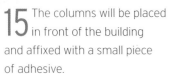

16 Attach the rotunda to the rest of the building by twisting the lower bubbles on the rotunda to the criss-crossed bubbles that are in the center of the rectangle.

17 Join those bubbles anywhere that seems convenient and provides a stable connection.

TIP

Due to the length of the bubbles in the base of the building, it may be difficult to keep them lined up without spaces forming. An adhesive such as rubber cement or double-sided tape will solve this problem.

18 A spire can be made for the top of the building with the last 160. Twist a series of bubbles and line them up against each other, leaving the small uninflated nipple at the end. Then just attach the spire to the top of the dome.

FULL OF HOT AIR

Several ghosts are believed to haunt the Capitol Building, including the mysterious Demon Cat.

FURTHER INFORMATION

By now you're probably anxious to further explore the world of balloon art. Everything from architecture and animals, to clothing and vehicles has been made from balloons. Think of a balloon as your paintbrush with which you can visualize and create, as with any other medium.

CHOOSING BALLOONS

There are many more types of balloon than you might imagine, from the small 160s used in this book, through six-foot round balloons that the author climbs into during his stage act. With just the right amount of air in it, and a bit of imagination, any balloon can be used to create art. Experiment with all the balloons you can find. Only this way can you identify your favorite type and brand. Some artists like thicker balloons. Others prefer thinner ones, which require less pressure to twist.

LIFESPAN OF BALLOON SCULPTURES

If left undisturbed, balloon sculptures will slowly deflate over time, usually holding their shape as they shrink and shrivel. Larger sculptures can still look good several weeks after they've been created! To ensure maximum longevity, keep your sculptures at a constant temperature and away from direct sunlight, while limiting handling of them.

There is an ongoing quest among many to make balloon sculptures last forever. However, the transient nature of the medium is one of the things that adds to its uniqueness and value. Balloon sculptures don't last forever, but the fun of creating them can last for years!

FURTHER READING

The following is a list of websites and recommended further reading for amateur and professional balloon artists alike.

WEBSITES

www.balloonHQ.com
largest source of balloon info

www.tmyers.com
balloon twisting material

www.balloonhat.com
balloon hats around the world

www.balloonmanor.com
haunted house made of balloons

www.balloonconvention.com
balloon twisting convention

BOOKS

Brilliant Balloon Modelling
(Top That Publishing PLC, 2005)
Balloon Sculpting: A Fun and Easy Guide to Making Balloon Animals, Toys and Games Bruce Fife
(Piccadilly Books, 2004)
Extreme Balloon Tying: More Than 40 Over-the-Top Projects
Shar Levine and Michael Ouchi
(Sterling, 2006)
Twisting History: Lessons in Balloon Sculpting Larry Moss
(Fooled Ya, 1995)

ABOUT THE AUTHOR

Larry Moss's accomplishments include the record for the largest non-round balloon sculpture in the world, using more than 40,000 balloons to construct two 40-foot tall soccer players. He also built the first and only piloted latex balloon sculpture, as well as a fully operational 100,000-balloon, 10,000 square-foot haunted house.

Renowned in his field for these large and technically challenging sculptures, Larry is also an experienced teacher of his art, as well as the author of several ballooning books. As the world's first self-proclaimed "airigamist," he also created, and continues to maintain, the largest balloon site on the Internet: BalloonHQ.com.

Make your own works of art with balloons.

Larry has a degree in applied math and computer science, as well as a master's in elementary education. His unusual career combines his love of teaching, entertaining and science. He has performed for audiences all over the world—from street corners and schools to rock concerts and television.

For more information, visit:
www.airigami.com.

Airigami: The art of folding air in specially prepared latex containers.

INDEX